OXFORD
UNIVERSITY PRESS

Wonders of the World

Contents

Moana Ashley

Mount Everest

Mountains are like very big hills. The tip of a mountain can be very cold. The highest mountain in the world is Mount Everest. Look at where Mount Everest is on the map. It is in Nepal.

Fact Box • *On top of Mount Everest it is hard to breathe.*

Great Barrier Reef

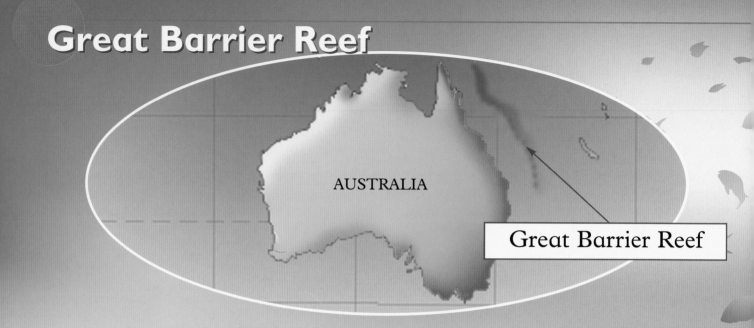

AUSTRALIA

Great Barrier Reef

A coral reef grows under the sea. Coral looks like plants but it is made by animals. The biggest coral reef in the world is the Great Barrier Reef in Australia. Look at where the Great Barrier Reef is on the map.

Fact Box • *Coral is a living thing. The Great Barrier Reef is growing.*

Greenland

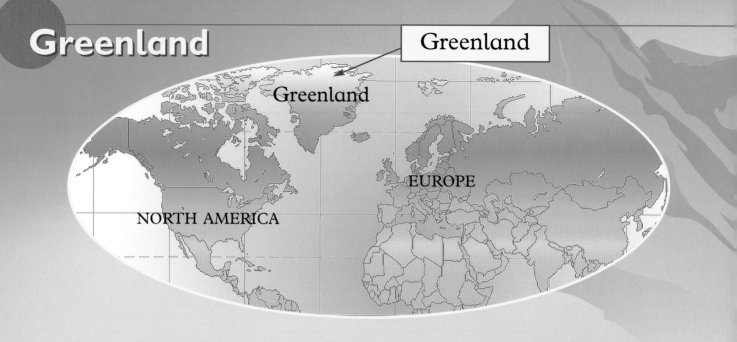

Greenland

Greenland

NORTH AMERICA

EUROPE

An island is a piece of land which has water all around it. Some islands are in the sea. Some islands are in lakes or rivers. Islands can be big or small. Greenland is the largest island in the world. Look at where Greenland is on the map.

Fact Box • Greenland is very cold. Snow falls every month of the year.

Lambert Glacier

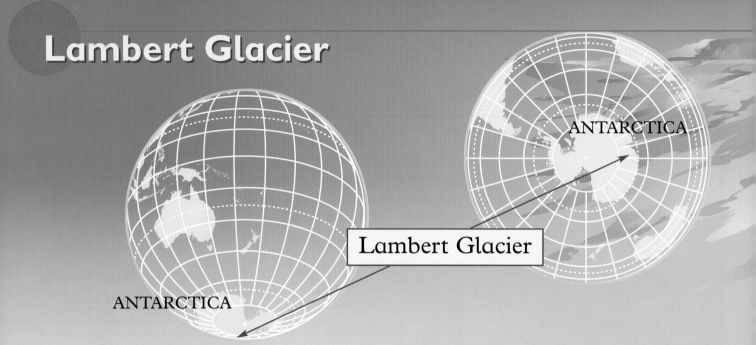

ANTARCTICA

Lambert Glacier

ANTARCTICA

A glacier is a very large lump of snow and ice. It moves along, but it moves so slowly that you cannot see it moving. The Lambert Glacier is the largest glacier in the world. It is in Antarctica.

Fact Box • *The Lambert Glacier is so cold that no one can live there.*

Jean Bernard Cave

United Kingdom

Germany

Jean Bernard Cave

France Switzerland

Italy

Spain

Caves are holes in rocks. Some of them are small. They do not go far into the rock. Some caves go deep into the rock. The deepest cave in the world is the Jean Bernard Cave in France.

Fact Box • The Jean Bernard Cave is a lot of caves joined together, with five ways in.

Angel Falls

When a river or stream runs over a cliff the water forms a waterfall. Sometimes, the water does not fall very far. Some waterfalls are very high, though. The water falls a long way. Angel Falls is the highest waterfall in the world. Look at where the Angel Falls is on the map.

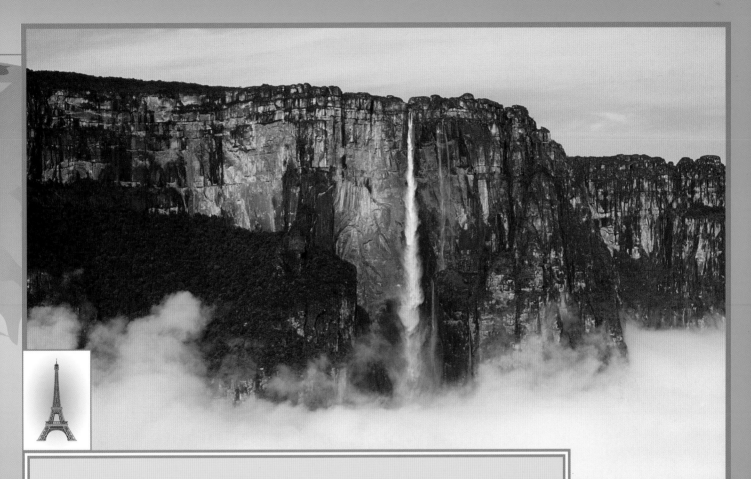

Fact Box • *The Angel Falls is more than three times the height of the Eiffel Tower in France.*

Sahara Desert

A desert is a place where there is very little rain.
There is not much water, and most plants
cannot grow. Deserts are often covered in sand.
The Sahara Desert is the largest desert in the
world. It is in northern Africa.

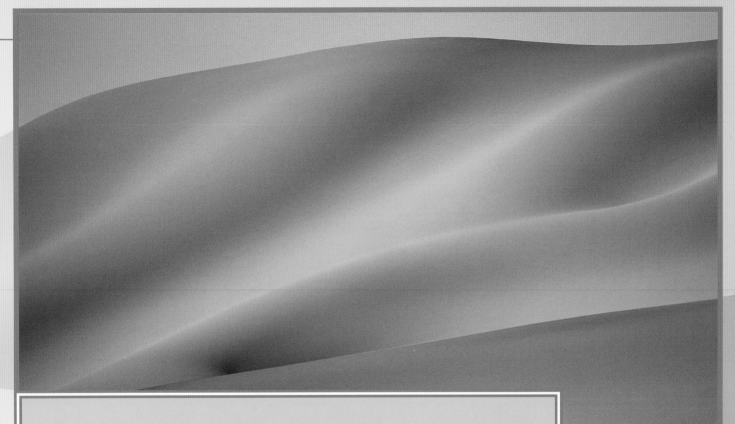

Fact Box • *The Sahara Desert is very hot and dry. The highest temperature ever recorded was in the Sahara Desert.*

Marianas Trench

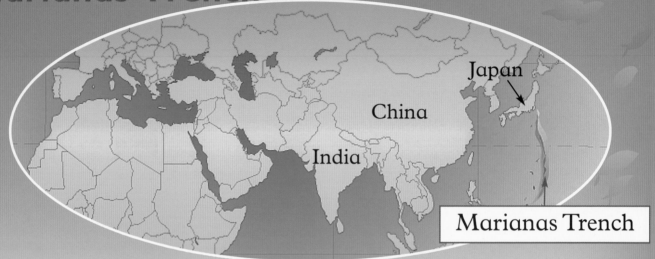

The sea can be very deep. The deepest place in the sea is called the Marianas Trench. In fact, it is the deepest place in the whole world! The Marianas Trench is 11,033 m deep. It is so deep you would need a submarine to get to the bottom.

Fact Box • *The Marianas Trench is so deep that no light can get to the bottom.*

Grand Canyon

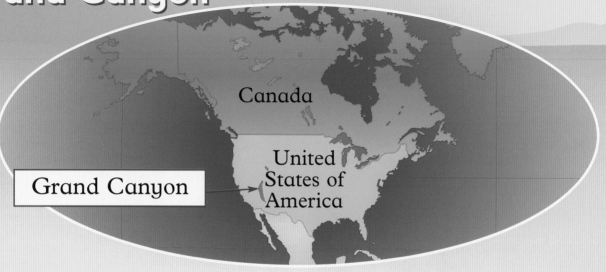

Canada

United States of America

Grand Canyon

A canyon is a long, deep valley in the earth. It is like a wide, deep crack. Sometimes, there is a river at the bottom of a canyon. The largest canyon in the world is the Grand Canyon in the United States of America.

Fact Box • The Grand Canyon is 1.6 km deep.

River Nile

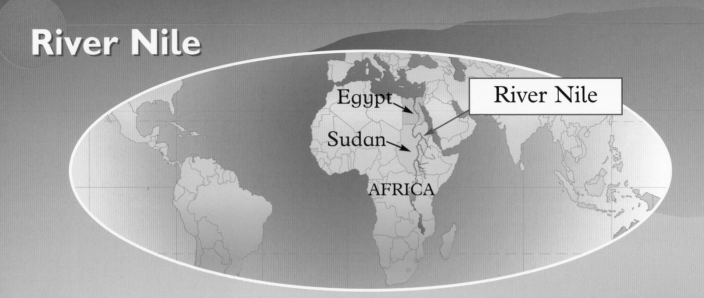

Egypt

Sudan

River Nile

AFRICA

The River Nile in Africa is the largest river in the world. Every year, there is so much rain that the river gets very deep and floods onto the land. When the water goes back into the river, it leaves earth and sand behind it. A lot of good food can be grown in this earth on the sides of the river.

Fact Box • Most of the food in Egypt is grown near the River Nile.

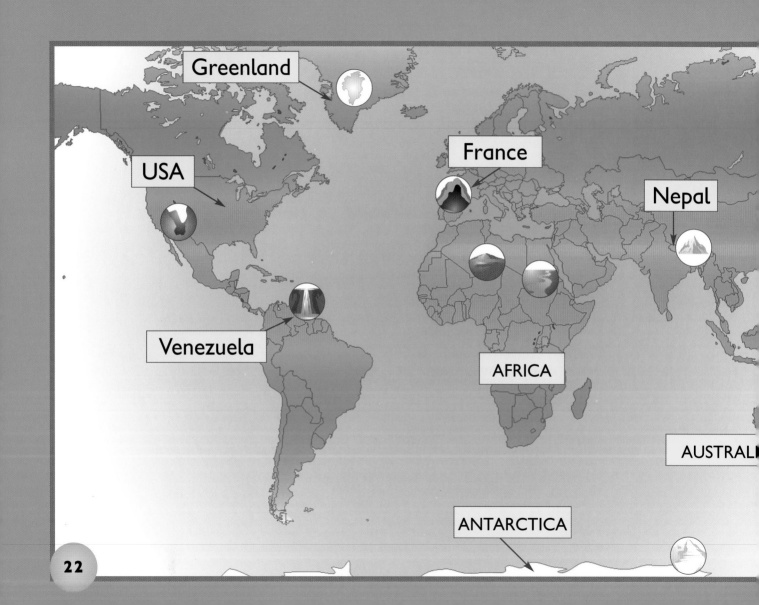

Greenland

France

USA

Nepal

Venezuela

AFRICA

AUSTRAL

ANTARCTICA

Pacific
Ocean

Can you find these Wonders of the World on the world map?

Key

 – Mount Everest

 – Great Barrier Reef

 – Greenland

 – Lambert Glacier

 – Jean Bernard Cave

 – Angel Falls

 – Sahara Desert

 – Marianas Trench

 – Grand Canyon

 – River Nile

Glossary

coral: The hard skeletons of sea animals.

desert: An area with little water, little vegetation and lots of sand.

trench: A long, deep, sunken ditch or hollow.

canyon: A long, deep valley, often with a river flowing through it.

glacier: A mass of ice, which is slowly moving.

reef: A strip of rock, coral or sand in the sea. A reef can be above or below the surface of the water.

submarine: A small boat that can go underwater.